Budgeting

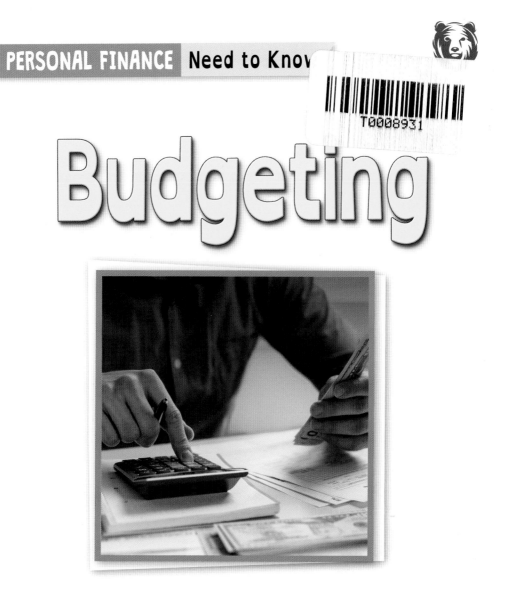

by Ruth Owen

Consultant: Kari Servais
Middle School Family & Consumer Science Educator

BEARPORT
PUBLISHING

Minneapolis, Minnesota

Credits

Cover and title page, © bymuratdeniz/iStock; 5T, © Stefano Chiacchiarini '74/Shutterstock; 5M, © Grisha Bruev/Shutterstock; 5B, © Freeograph/Shutterstock; 7, © Dobo Kristian/Shutterstock; 9, © BearFotos/Shutterstock; 10–11, © ZikG/Shutterstock; 11, © Ray Bond/Shutterstock; 13, © Deepak Sethi/iStock; 15, © pathdoc/Shutterstock; 17, © Prostock-studio/Shutterstock; 19, © LADO/Shutterstock; 21, © Pressmaster/Shutterstock; 23, © YinYang/iStock; 25T, © guvendemir/iStock; 25B, © treerawat_Kun/Shutterstock; and 27, © Mangostar/Shutterstock.

Bearport Publishing Company Product Development Team

President: Jen Jenson; Director of Product Development: Spencer Brinker; Senior Editor: Allison Juda; Editor: Charly Haley; Associate Editor: Naomi Reich; Senior Designer: Colin O'Dea; Associate Designer: Elena Klinkner; Associate Designer: Kayla Eggert; Product Development Assistant: Anita Stasson

Library of Congress Cataloging-in-Publication Data

Names: Owen, Ruth, 1967– author.
Title: Budgeting / Ruth Owen.
Description: Silvertip books. | Minneapolis, Minnesota : Bearport
   Publishing Company, [2023] | Series: Personal finance: need to know |
   Includes bibliographical references and index.
Identifiers: LCCN 2022032864 (print) | LCCN 2022032865 (ebook) | ISBN
   9798885094153 (library binding) | ISBN 9798885095372 (paperback) | ISBN
   9798885096522 (ebook)
Subjects: LCSH: Budget–Juvenile literature. | Money–Juvenile literature.
   | Finance, Personal–Juvenile literature.
Classification: LCC HJ2005 .O854 2023 (print) | LCC HJ2005 (ebook) | DDC
   352.4/8–dc23/eng/20220711
LC record available at https://lccn.loc.gov/2022032864
LC ebook record available at https://lccn.loc.gov/2022032865

For more information, write to Bearport Publishing, 5357 Penn Avenue South, Minneapolis, MN 55419.

Budgeting is all about making a plan for your money. You might make a budget for a week, a month, or even longer. The budget should start with your **income**, or the money you earn. Then, subtract how much you expect to spend during that time.

While budgeting, people think about when they need to pay for things. If someone buys groceries every week, that cost goes in a weekly budget. A monthly budget may include rent or car payments.

Do I Need It or Want It?

The spending part of a budget may include money for both needs and wants. A responsible budget takes care of the needs first. If you need to replace shoes you've outgrown, buy those first. After that, you can spend money on something fun.

Which wants are in your budget? There might be an app subscription or a trip to a theme park. These things make life more fun, but we don't need them to survive.

Nice Save!

Along with money to spend, budgets may set aside some money to save. Saving may be for a specific goal. Some people save for something big, such as their first car. Having savings is also helpful in emergencies.

What happens if your phone breaks? If you have savings in your budget, you will have money for unexpected spending. You can get your phone fixed.

Stay on Track

People plan their budgets carefully. But things don't always go according to plan. There may be an unexpected problem that was not in the budget. If someone loses their job, their income changes. Good budgets help people keep track of their money and costs, even when things change.

Special websites and apps can make tracking budgets easy! All you need to do is enter your income and spending. Then, keep an eye on whether you stay on budget.

A Balancing Act

Tracking a budget is all about balance. In a balanced budget, the income is the same as the spending. If you spend more than you earn, your budget is not balanced. It has a **deficit**. That means you are in debt.

If your budget has a deficit, you might be able to work more to increase your income. You could also try spending less. Buying fewer things or cheaper things may help you cut spending.

Sometimes, a budget that isn't balanced can be a good thing! If you earn more than you spend, you will have extra money. This is called a **surplus**. Surplus money can be saved for later or spent on wants.

When a budget has a deficit, we say it is in the red. If a budget has a surplus, it's called in the black.

Be a Smart Shopper

How do people stick to their budgets? One way is to shop carefully by comparing prices. People may look at different **brands** or even visit several stores to find the best prices for things. Many people compare prices online, too.

If you don't need something right away, you could try waiting for a sale. Buying it at the lower sale price will save money. You can use coupons for lower prices, too.

A Household Budget

There are many different kinds of budgets. A **household** budget may be for a person living alone or for a family. Often, a big part of the budget will go toward paying for the home. Other costs will include **bills** for services. Most households pay for electricity, heat, water, and internet.

Some people track all their money in their household budget. But some include only what they plan to spend on their home. Then, they have separate budgets for spending money on other things.

Bigger Budgets

Businesses and organizations need budgets, too. This includes everything from schools to grocery stores. These budgets usually change over time. When a company builds a new store, its budget may include buying the land and construction materials. Once the store is open, it needs to budget for things to sell.

A store makes money from selling its products. This income must be at least equal to the cost of all spending. A store's spending can include paying for electricity, heating, and workers.

Even countries have budgets. Much of a government's income comes from **taxes** that people pay. This money is spent on the needs of everyone in the country. It helps pay for everything from running the military to maintaining national parks.

Taxes go to city and state governments, too. Each government has its own budget. City budgets may pay for fire departments and clean water. State budgets cover fixing state roadways and more.

Plan, Spend, Save

Budgeting may seem like a lot of work, but it's worth it. Setting a budget helps you get the most out of your money. You can plan to buy things you need, save for emergencies, and spend on something fun!

Many people donate money. While budgeting, people may set aside money so they can give to **charities** and causes they care about.

Balancing a Monthly Budget

How does someone keep their budget balanced? Their income must equal the amount of money they spend and save. Let's look at an example.

INCOME
All the money coming in

JOB	AMOUNT	NOTES
Mow the lawn	$10	Chore
Vacuum the house	$10	Chore
Do the dishes	$10	Chore
Babysitting	$25	Job for a neighbor
Total income:	**$55**	

SPENDING
The money to pay for things

THINGS TO BUY	AMOUNT	NOTES
Bus fare	$2	To get to babysitting
Shampoo	$5	
Notebook	$3	For English class
Visit to water park	$10	Fun with friends
New T-shirt	$10	New clothes
Give money to animal charity	$5	
Total spending:	**$35**	

SAVINGS GOALS
Money set aside for something later

JOB	AMOUNT	NOTES
Save for cool shoes	$5	
Save for first car	$10	Grandma will match what I save!
Save for emergencies	$5	
Total savings:	**$20**	

SilverTips for SUCCESS

★ SilverTips for REVIEW

Review what you've learned. Use the text to help you.

Define key terms

budgeting   saving

income   wants

needs

Check for understanding

What is a balanced budget?

How can someone keep track of their budget?

Why might a person include saving in their budget?

Think deeper

Think about the things in your life that cost money. If you made a budget, which of these things should you be sure to pay for first?

★ SilverTips on TEST-TAKING

- **Make a study plan.** Ask your teacher what the test is going to cover. Then, set aside time to study a little bit every day.

- **Read all the questions carefully.** Be sure you know what is being asked.

- **Skip any questions** you don't know how to answer right away. Mark them and come back later if you have time.

Glossary

bills documents that show how much money is owed for something

brands names that group products by the companies that make them

budgeting making a plan for your money that includes income and spending

charities groups that raise money or run programs for those in need

deficit a situation where more money has been spent than earned

household a home, the people who live there, and all the things in that space

income the money a person makes from their job

surplus a situation where more money has been earned than spent

taxes money paid by people to their government

Read More

Hill, Christina. *Budgeting in Infographics (Econo-Graphics).* Ann Arbor, MI: Cherry Lake Publishing, 2023.

Huddleston, Emma. *Living on a Budget (Money Basics).* San Diego, CA: BrightPoint Press, 2020.

Uhl, Xina M. and Judy Monroe Peterson. *Making a Budget (Managing Your Money and Finances).* New York: Rosen Publishing, 2020.

Learn More Online

1. Go to **www.factsurfer.com** or scan the QR code below.

2. Enter "**Budgeting**" into the search box.

3. Click on the cover of this book to see a list of websites.

Index

About the Author

Ruth Owen has written hundreds of non-fiction books. She lives on the Cornish coast in England with her husband and three cats.